Communication Skills

by Mari Schuh

PEBBLE
a capstone imprint

Pebble Explore is published by Pebble, an imprint of Capstone
1710 Roe Crest Drive
North Mankato, Minnesota 56003
www.capstonepub.com

**Library of Congress Cataloging-in-Publication Data is available on
the Library of Congress website.**
ISBN: 978-1-9771-3217-8 (library binding)
ISBN: 978-1-9771-3319-9 (paperback)
ISBN: 978-1-9771-5404-0 (ebook PDF)

Summary: Communication is the sharing of information. It sounds
easy, but that's not always the case. Did you know your body
language and the tone of your voice are just as important as what you
are saying? Learn to communicate with confidence in every situation.

Image Credits
iStockphoto: kali9, 29; LightFieldStudios, 26; SDI Productions,
13; Shutterstock: Andy Dean Photography, Cover; ANURAK
PONGPATIMET, 27; Brocreative, 19; EZ-Stock Studio, 21; fizkes, 6;
Jsnow my wolrd, 8; Monkey Business Images, 9, 16-17, 23; naluwan,
7; NDAB Creativity, 10; photonova, design element throughout;
PR Image Factory, 22; Rido, 15, 24; Robert Kneschke, 5; Syda
Productions, 25

Editorial Credits
Editor: Christianne Jones; Designer: Sarah Bennett; Media Researcher:
Morgan Walters; Production Specialist: Laura Manthe

All internet sites appearing in back matter were available and
accurate when this book was sent to press.

Table of Contents

Bold words are in the glossary.

Sharing Feelings and Ideas

Have you been in touch with your friends today? Did you talk in person or on the phone? Maybe you listened to a friend tell a story. Maybe you wrote a note or sent a text message.

Talking, listening, and writing are **communication** skills. These skills help you have good **relationships**. When do you use these skills? Every day!

These skills help you give and receive information. You tell people what you think. You share your ideas and feelings. You learn how others are feeling.

Communication is a series of steps. People send a message. Others receive it. They read, hear, or see the message. Then they work to understand the message.

There are a lot of ways to communicate. You call your mom. You send a note or email to a friend. You listen to your teacher.

Sometimes lots of people get a message. Thousands of people watch and hear a news report on TV. Sometimes only one person receives a message. Evan whispers to a friend.

Talking

A big part of communication is talking. It's good to speak up! You can talk about things that are important to you. You can say what is going on in your life.

Let others know how you are feeling. Be honest. Maybe you are tired or are not feeling well. You can tell your friends that you don't feel like playing today. By telling your friends the reason why, you help them understand.

When you talk, it's good to talk slowly. Try to be calm. Don't rush. People might not understand your words if you talk too quickly.

Try to think before you talk. When you're stressed or upset, you might say something you don't really mean to say. So, take your time to think about what you want to say. Pause between sentences. This gives you and others time to think.

When you're done talking, let the person ask questions. Then answer the best way you can.

Be polite when you talk. Use words that are respectful. Calling someone a bad name can cause hurt feelings. Also remember to say please and thank you. Think about how your words sound. If you talk too loudly, you might sound angry.

Rafai says hi to her bus driver every day. She asks her how she's doing. Rafai smiles as she talks.

Listening

Listening is an important skill. Listening can be more important than talking! Why? It helps you learn. It helps you get information. Listening is a way to show people that you care.

Listening is not easy. It takes energy. You have to think to listen. It can be hard to listen for a long time. But try your best. Listen to everything a person is saying. If you stop listening, you will miss out.

Good listeners are **alert**. They pay attention. They look at the person who is talking. They **focus** on what the person is saying. Good listeners put away toys and phones. They are not distracted.

Jael listens to his teacher. He looks at his teacher as he talks. Jael hears his teacher explain the lesson. Jael focuses on his teacher. He is not distracted by kids in the hallway.

As a good listener, you need to be patient. Try not to **interrupt**, even if you are excited. Don't talk until it is your turn. Listen carefully. This shows respect. It shows you **value** what the other person is saying.

Tasha listens to her friend Jill talk about her new puppy. Tasha is excited to tell Jill about summer camp. But Tasha waits. Tasha listens to Jill. Tasha is a good listener. Then Tasha asks Jill questions about her puppy.

Good listeners understand that people like different things. They have different ideas and feelings. Good listeners want to learn about other people.

As you listen, think about what other people are saying. Take time to think about how they feel. Try to understand how they feel. When they are done talking, ask questions. This way, you can be sure you truly understand what they said.

Body Language

People can learn how you are feeling without you saying one word! How? Your body and face can tell them.

Your face might look sad if you don't like what someone is saying. You might cross your arms. Maybe you tap your feet. Or you might look away.

It's good to look at the person who is talking to you. Smile. Sit up. Lean forward a bit as you listen. Your body language shows you are interested. It shows you are paying attention.

Writing

Writing is another important communication skill. It can be a good way to share ideas and thoughts. Some people write on paper. Others use computers. They might write email messages. Or they might send text messages on their phones.

People write about their ideas. Sara writes her project ideas in her science notebook. People write down information to help them remember. Hanie's dad writes a grocery list. People also write about their feelings. Harry writes in his journal every night before bed.

The more you write, the easier it will be. Write a letter to your grandma. Write a note to your neighbor. Write a story about your best friend. Make lists of things you like to do.

Being a good reader will help you be a good writer. You will learn new words and get new ideas. Read to a stuffed animal. Read with your sister. Read to a pet. Just read.

Always Learning

Being good at listening, talking, and writing takes time. You can practice these skills. You can make them a **habit**. Try to read and write every day.

Set a **goal** to be a better listener. Listen carefully. Learn how to ask good questions. Learn how to say what you really want to say.

Take time to think before you talk. These skills will help you as you grow up. They will make you a better student and a better friend.

Glossary

alert (uh-LURT)—awake and paying attention

communication (kuh-myoo-nuh-KAY-shuhn)—the sharing of facts, ideas, or feelings with other people

focus (FOH-kuss)—to keep all your attention

goal (GOHL)—something that you aim for or work toward

habit (HAB-it)—something that you do often

interrupt (in-tuh-RUHPT)—to start talking before someone else has finished talking

relationship (ri-LAY-shuhn-ship)—the way in which people get along with one another

value (VAL-yoo)—to believe that something is important

Read More

Cooper, Scott. *Speak Up and Get Along!* Minneapolis: Free Spirit Publishing, 2019.

Metzger, Steve. *Yes, I Can Listen!* Chicago: Parenting Press, 2019.

Salaka, Michael. *Why Do We Have to Listen to People We Disagree With?* New York: PowerKids Press, 2019.

Internet Sites

BrainPOP: Conflict Resolution
www.brainpop.com/health/conflictresolution/
conflictresolution

Kids' Health: Getting Along with Others
www.cyh.com/HealthTopics/HealthTopicDetailsKids.
aspx?p=335&np=289&id=3051

KidsHealth: Talking About Your Feelings
kidshealth.org/en/kids/talk-feelings.html

Index